I0449020

THE

48 LAWS OF EMOTIONAL

M
A
N
I
P
U
L
A
T
I
O
N

Author

Cameron Dallas

Publisher's Note

This document provides accurate and reliable information on the subject. Because the publisher is not required to provide accounting, licensed, or qualified services, the publication is sold. Order a legal or professional expert for advice.

Copying, printing, or transmitting this document is illegal. Recording and storing this publication without written permission from the publisher is prohibited. Rights reserved.

The reader is solely responsible for any liability resulting from using or abusing policies, processes, or directions in this document.

The publisher is not liable for any damages, losses, or reparations caused by the information herein.

Copyright © 2023 Cameron Dallas

Copyright fuels creativity, encourages diverse voices, promotes free speech, and creates a vibrant culture. Thank you for buying a copy of this book.

Note to Readers.

Note that this book provides different experiences about life with easy understanding.

ISBN: 978-1-312-17637-9

CONTENTS

INTRODUCTION

EMOTIONAL MANIPULATION

Emotional manipulation, an intricate dance of psychology and influence, is a phenomenon that traverses the realms of relationships, communication, and human behavior. In this foundational chapter, we embark on a journey to dissect the essence of emotional manipulation—unveiling its mechanisms, exploring its motivations, and delving into its effects on manipulators and those who fall under their sway.

UNMASKING MANIPULATION

Peeling back the layers, we uncover the various masks manipulation wears—sometimes camouflaged in kindness, others shrouded in charm. We decipher the underlying motives driving manipulative behavior, be it power, control, or the desire for personal gain. By recognizing these motives, we lay the groundwork for understanding the complex web of emotions that manipulators exploit.

PSYCHOLOGY OF INFLUENCE

Diving into the psychology of influence, we examine the cognitive biases, social dynamics, and emotional triggers that manipulators deftly manipulate to their advantage. This exploration unravels the intricate interplay between emotions, beliefs, and behaviors that lay the foundation for manipulation's success.

IMPACT ON TARGETS

Without understanding its profound impact on targets, no discussion of emotional manipulation is complete. We explore the emotional rollercoaster victims often endure, ranging from confusion and self-doubt to helplessness. By grasping the psychological toll of manipulation, we gain insight into how to recognize and counter its effects.

THE MANIPULATOR'S TOOLKIT

A glimpse into the manipulator's toolkit reveals an arsenal of tactics ranging from guilt-tripping to gaslighting. By dissecting these tactics, we arm ourselves with the knowledge that empowers us to detect and resist manipulation, enhancing our emotional resilience and personal agency.

ETHICS AND AWARENESS

As we navigate this terrain, we're compelled to question the ethical boundaries of manipulation. We reflect on instances where persuasion transitions into deceit and contemplate the importance of awareness as a defense mechanism against emotional manipulation.

Through understanding emotional manipulation, we equip ourselves with a mental armor that safeguards against the subtle ploys of manipulators. This chapter serves as a compass, guiding us through the labyrinthine pathways of human emotions and interactions, offering insight into the forces shaping our relationships and responses to them.

PART I
LAYING THE FOUNDATION

THE POWER OF EMOTIONAL MANIPULATION

Emotions, the driving force behind human behavior, hold an incredible power—both to connect and to control. In this chapter, we delve into the intricate dynamics that make emotional manipulation a potent force, exploring how emotions can be harnessed to manipulate others while also shedding light on the ethical considerations that come into play.

UNVEILING EMOTIONAL VULNERABILITIES

In all their raw authenticity, emotions are the touchstones of human vulnerability. Here, we unveil the power of recognizing and exploiting these vulnerabilities—how manipulators deftly identify emotional triggers and wield them to bend others to their will. We examine the delicate balance between empathy and exploitation, unveiling the profound impact emotional manipulation can have on individuals' choices and actions.

INFLUENCE THROUGH EMOTIONAL CONNECTION

Emotional bonds are the glue that holds relationships together. This section explores how manipulators masterfully build and exploit these bonds, using shared experiences, memories, and emotions to exert control. We delve into the psychology of attachment and the magnetic pull that draws individuals deeper into the manipulator's web.

THE ILLUSION OF CHOICE

Within the realm of emotional manipulation lies a subtle dance that tricks individuals into believing they're making choices of their own accord. We explore how manipulators nudge decisions by carefully orchestrating emotional highs and lows, rendering targets more susceptible to influence. This section exposes the art of steering emotions to reshape perceptions and outcomes.

THE RIPPLE EFFECT

The power of emotional manipulation goes beyond the immediate interaction, rippling through relationships, organizations, and societies. We investigate case studies illuminating the far-reaching consequences of emotional manipulation, highlighting its potential to reshape narratives, beliefs, and even history.

HARNESSING EMPATHY AND COMPASSION

Ethics and responsibility come to the forefront as we consider the manipulation of emotions like empathy and compassion. We reflect on the potential for good and harm as these emotions are harnessed, and we ponder the fine line between using emotional influence to uplift and inspire versus using it to deceive and control.

RECOGNIZING MANIPULATIVE BEHAVIOR

In the intricate dance of human interactions, recognizing the signs of manipulation is akin to deciphering a cryptic code. This chapter empowers readers with the discernment needed to identify manipulative behavior, laying the groundwork for building resilience and safeguarding against the subtle tactics wielded by those seeking to exert control.

THE WEB OF DECEPTION

Manipulative behavior thrives in the shadows, often masquerading as genuine concern or camaraderie. We delve into the deceptive façades that manipulators adopt, revealing the veiled motives that drive their actions. By unveiling the mismatch between words and intentions, we empower ourselves to pierce through the intricate web of deceit.

BEHAVIORAL PATTERNS AND RED FLAGS

In this section, we explore the recurring behavioral patterns that betray the presence of manipulation. From inconsistency in actions to overtly exploiting emotions, we identify the red flags that act as warning signals. With the knowledge of these patterns, readers can recognize manipulation as it unfolds.

GASLIGHTING AND DISTORTION

A deeper dive into gaslighting—the art of distorting reality—sheds light on one of the most insidious forms of manipulation. We examine how manipulators skillfully create doubt, confusion, and self-questioning, leaving their targets emotionally disarmed. By understanding the tactics of gaslighting, readers gain the tools to reclaim their sense of reality.

INTUITION AND EMPOWERMENT

Intuition often serves as an invaluable compass in navigating the complex landscape of relationships. This section encourages readers to trust their gut feelings and instincts, offering guidance on honing intuitive awareness to recognize manipulation even in its most subtle forms. By nurturing this intuition, readers fortify their emotional defenses.

THE IMPORTANCE OF BOUNDARIES

Recognizing manipulation necessitates a strong sense of personal boundaries. We explore the interplay between boundaries and manipulation, discussing how manipulators exploit the lack thereof. Through understanding the role of limitations in deterring manipulation, readers discover the empowerment that comes from defining and upholding their limits.

SEEKING SUPPORT AND VALIDATION

Navigating the world of manipulation can be isolating, leaving victims feeling uncertain and alone. This section emphasizes the importance of seeking support and validation from trusted sources.

By sharing experiences and seeking guidance, readers harness the collective wisdom that bolsters their ability to recognize manipulation and respond effectively.

Through recognizing manipulative behavior, we don the armor of awareness that shields us from the invisible ploys of manipulators. This chapter serves as a guidebook to deciphering the cryptic language of manipulation, enabling readers to reclaim agency over their emotions and choices while fostering healthier, more authentic relationships.

PART II
LAWS FOR MANIPULATIVE INFLUENCE

LAW I

APPEALING TO EMOTIONS

Law I explores the concept of using emotions as a strategic tool in the art of emotional manipulation. It emphasizes the power of appealing to emotions to influence how others perceive things and make decisions. Manipulators are skilled at using the powerful force of emotions to effectively manipulate people and influence their behavior. They understand how human psychology works and use this knowledge to create a situation that is favorable to achieving their goals.

UNDERSTANDING THE LAW

The essence of this law is based on the understanding that emotions play a significant role in influencing human behavior. Manipulators can influence people by appealing to their emotions. They do this by understanding and exploiting the natural desires, fears, and aspirations that individuals have. By manipulating these emotions, they can shape them in a way that serves their agenda. The law being referred to here is one that brings attention to the use of emotions such as empathy, compassion, sympathy, and guilt as tools for influencing and controlling others.

CASE STUDY: THE SCHEMING SYMPATHIZER

In this workplace scenario, there is a coworker who often talks about their challenges and difficulties. This person has a talent for skillfully crafting stories that evoke feelings of sadness, which resonates with their colleagues and elicits their empathy. Over time, the colleagues of this individual offer help, take on tasks that were not completed on time, and even support and advocate for their ideas to alleviate their perceived difficulties. This coworker, without their knowledge, uses emotional appeals to gain strong support and promote their agenda.

COUNTERING THE MANIPULATION

Recognizing the manipulation at play is the first step in countering its effects. Individuals must cultivate self-awareness, allowing them to differentiate genuine emotions from those being strategically employed to influence decisions. By pausing to analyze their responses, individuals can make choices that align with their values and objectives rather than reacting impulsively to emotional appeals.

The importance of using critical thinking and emotional intelligence is highlighted when it comes to handling manipulation. Developing a greater level of awareness is possible when individuals can understand and interpret the complex network of emotional appeals. Being aware of these tactics can help individuals avoid becoming unwittingly involved in manipulative situations where people use emotions to influence others.

LAW 2

CREATING A SENSE OF DEPENDENCE

Law 2 explores the concept of emotional manipulation and how it can be used strategically to gain control over others. It focuses specifically on fostering a sense of dependence to exert this control. Manipulators use a strategy of creating a network of dependence and interconnectedness to take advantage of the vulnerability that comes with relying on others. This allows them to establish themselves as essential individuals in the lives of their victims.

DECIPHERING THE LAW

At the heart of this law lies the recognition that dependence breeds vulnerability. Manipulators capitalize on this vulnerability, employing tactics that blur the lines between autonomy and reliance. This law explores the intricacies of creating emotional, psychological, or practical dependence, thereby ensuring that targets perceive the manipulator as an indispensable source of support or guidance.

CASE STUDY: THE MENTOR'S STRINGS

In this scenario, there is a mentor who is actively supporting and guiding the growth and development of a protégé within a professional environment. The mentor gradually influences decisions in a subtle manner, which ultimately leads the protégé to rely on their guidance for achieving success. The mentor guides the protégé in a way that makes them rely on the mentor and directs their path toward the mentor's goals. When someone becomes a protégé, they often find themselves relying heavily on their mentor. This reliance can sometimes lead to a situation where the protégé sacrifices their ability to make decisions and take control of their own life.

COUNTERING THE MANIPULATION

Recognizing the establishment of dependence is key to countering its influence. Individuals must cultivate self-reliance and an awareness of the dynamics at play in their relationships. By fostering a balance between collaboration and independence, they can avoid becoming ensnared in relationships marked by unequal power dynamics.

This emphasizes the significance of nurturing a healthy interdependence in relationships. It is crucial to prioritize collaboration that is built upon mutual respect, rather than resorting to manipulative tactics. When individuals have a deep understanding of how dependence is formed, they can better navigate the complex world of emotional manipulation. This understanding allows them to make more informed decisions, protecting their independence and ability to make choices for themselves.

LAW 3

ORCHESTRATING EMOTIONAL HIGHS AND LOWS

Law 3 explores the concept of strategically creating emotional peaks and valleys to influence how people perceive and behave. Manipulators can effectively utilize the emotional states of others to their advantage. They do this by creating a series of fluctuating feelings, similar to a rollercoaster ride, which keeps their targets feeling uncertain and vulnerable. This makes the targets more easily influenced by the manipulator.

UNVEILING THE LAW

Central to this law is the understanding that emotions are not static but rather dynamic states that can be guided. Manipulators adeptly employ this principle, inducing emotional peaks and valleys to foster dependency and control. This law explores the psychology of emotional oscillation, shedding light on how manipulators amplify positive emotions and exploit vulnerability during lows.

CASE STUDY: THE ROMANTIC PUPPETEER

In this scenario, picture a romantic relationship where one partner skillfully moves between intense displays of love and moments of emotional distance. During moments of closeness and emotional connection, the manipulator intentionally enhances feelings of happiness and pleasure, which in turn strengthens the emotional bond between them and their target. In this situation, the person intentionally creates situations where they create emotional distance between themselves and their partner. This causes the partner to doubt their value and desperately try to reconnect with them. The manipulator can maintain control over their partner's emotions and actions by strategically creating both positive and negative emotional experiences.

COUNTERING THE MANIPULATION

Recognizing the pattern of emotional oscillation is crucial to counter its impact. Individuals must cultivate emotional resilience, learning to differentiate genuine emotions from those artificially induced. By maintaining a steady emotional baseline and seeking partners who prioritize mutual respect and emotional stability, individuals can avoid falling into manipulative cycles.

Emotional awareness and stability play a crucial role in relationships, highlighting their importance. When individuals learn how to effectively manage and control their emotions, they gain the ability to escape from manipulative behaviors. This allows them to form healthier relationships based on genuine feelings and emotional stability.

LAW 4

EXPLOITING VULNERABILITIES

Law 4 explores the concept of taking advantage of weaknesses to influence people. Manipulators can create a situation where others become dependent on them and comply with their wishes by identifying and taking advantage of their weaknesses. This allows manipulators to control and influence their targets to achieve the outcomes they desire.

DECIPHERING THE LAW

The fundamental principle underlying this law is the recognition that vulnerabilities possess the potential to be transformed into strategic leverage points to exert control. Manipulators possess the ability to discern and exploit the emotional, psychological, and personal vulnerabilities of their targets, leveraging this understanding to exert control and influence over them. This legislation explores the psychological aspects of vulnerability and highlights how individuals who manipulate others take advantage of these vulnerabilities to exert control and influence.

CASE STUDY: THE EMOTIONAL BLACKMAILER

In the given scenario, we can explore a situation where an individual's close friend unintentionally stumbles upon a personal secret belonging to another friend. The manipulator strategically exploits the sensitivity of the situation, leveraging this vulnerability as a means of negotiation. The individual employs subtle insinuations that suggest the potential disclosure of a secret unless specific favors or concessions are provided. This tactic poses a considerable risk to the target's reputation and interpersonal connections. Through the exploitation of vulnerabilities, manipulators can achieve their objectives by employing emotional coercion tactics.

COUNTERING THE MANIPULATION

Recognizing the manipulation of vulnerabilities is crucial for counteracting its impact. Individuals must cultivate self-awareness, identify their vulnerabilities, and understand the tactics used by manipulators. By seeking support from trusted sources and setting clear boundaries, individuals can shield themselves from manipulation based on their weaknesses.

The significance of personal empowerment and resilience in the context of manipulation is emphasized. By gaining an understanding of how vulnerabilities can be exploited, individuals can better navigate their relationships and interactions with a heightened sense of discernment. This knowledge helps to ensure that their weaknesses are not manipulated by individuals who aim to exert control over them.

LAW 5

FEIGNING HELPLESSNESS

Law 5 explores the tactic of pretending to be helpless to gain sympathy and receive help from others. Manipulators strategically portray themselves as incapable or in need of gaining an advantage over their targets. This tactic allows them to create a power dynamic that heavily favors their control.

UNMASKING THE LAW

Central to this law is the recognition that portraying oneself as helpless engenders sympathy and a desire to assist. Manipulators exploit this dynamic by casting themselves as victims, invoking compassion from others. This law explores the psychological mechanisms behind feigned helplessness, showcasing how manipulators manipulate empathy to their advantage.

CASE STUDY: THE INGENIOUS MARTYR

Consider a hypothetical situation in which an individual consistently presents themselves as overwhelmed and lacking the ability to effectively navigate the various challenges that life presents. Individuals exhibiting this behavior often display a consistent pattern of seeking ongoing assistance and support from their social circle, including friends, family, and colleagues. They tend to position themselves as the perpetual victim, consistently portraying themselves as being in a state of disadvantage or suffering. In actuality, these individuals strategically adopt a pretense of helplessness to garner attention, favors, and influence over the decisions of others.

COUNTERING THE MANIPULATION

Recognizing the manipulation of feigned helplessness is key to countering its effects. Individuals must cultivate discernment, distinguishing between genuine need and manipulative tactics. By setting healthy boundaries and encouraging self-sufficiency in others, they can navigate relationships based on mutual respect rather than one-sided dependence.

This approach underscores the significance of combining empathy with critical thinking. By gaining a deep understanding of the complex dynamics involved in feigned helplessness, individuals can develop the necessary skills to offer authentic support while also protecting themselves from becoming entangled in relationships characterized by manipulation and unequal power dynamics.

PART III

LAWS FOR SHAPING
PERCEPTIONS

LAW 6

CRAFTING A DESIRED IMAGE

Law 6 explores the concept of creating a specific image to influence how others perceive you and to have control over the stories that are told about you. Manipulators have a strategic approach to how they present themselves, carefully shaping the way others perceive them and positioning themselves as authoritative figures.

DECIPHERING THE LAW

At the heart of this law lies the recognition that perception is malleable, and manipulators wield this truth to their advantage. By projecting a carefully curated image, they create an aura of credibility and influence. This law explores the psychology of image crafting, shedding light on how manipulators manipulate others' perceptions to suit their objectives.

CASE STUDY: THE CHARISMATIC LEADER

Imagine a charismatic leader who portrays themselves as compassionate, visionary, and dedicated to the well-being of their followers. Through charismatic communication and calculated actions, they build an image of moral authority and integrity. In reality, this image is skillfully crafted to consolidate power and maintain followers' loyalty, effectively manipulating their perceptions.

COUNTERING THE MANIPULATION

Recognizing the manipulation of crafted images is crucial to countering its effects. Individuals must cultivate critical thinking, scrutinizing actions and behaviors rather than being swayed solely by appearances. By seeking diverse perspectives and conducting independent research, they can uncover the gaps between projected images and genuine intent.

Discernment plays a crucial role when confronted with image manipulation. Through a comprehensive comprehension of the techniques involved in creating desired visual representations, individuals can enhance their ability to interact with others genuinely and critically. This enables them to establish meaningful connections based on depth and sincerity, rather than superficiality. Additionally, this proficiency allows individuals to question and scrutinize narratives that may be deceptive or misleading, thereby promoting a more accurate understanding of reality.

LAW 7

CONTROLLING INFORMATION FLOW

Law 7 explores the manipulation tactic of controlling information flow to gain advantage and assert influence. Manipulators strategically control what information is shared, when it is shared, and with whom it is shared, effectively shaping the perceptions and decisions of their targets.

UNVEILING THE LAW

Central to this law is the understanding that information is a powerful currency in human interactions. Manipulators control the narrative by selectively revealing or concealing information to steer perceptions and outcomes. This law delves into the psychology of information control, showcasing how manipulators manipulate access to knowledge to their advantage.

CASE STUDY: THE CONCEALING CONFIDANT

Consider a hypothetical situation in which an individual possesses crucial knowledge regarding the actions of a colleague that could have a substantial impact on the latter's professional trajectory. The confidant makes a deliberate decision to withhold this information from the colleague, while subtly divulging it to other individuals. The strategic control of information flow grants the individual with insider knowledge a distinct advantage, allowing them to subtly influence decisions and manipulate outcomes.

COUNTERING THE MANIPULATION

Recognizing the manipulation of information flow is vital for countering its effects. Individuals must cultivate a thirst for truth and objective understanding, seeking multiple sources and perspectives. By fostering a culture of transparent communication and encouraging open dialogue, they can mitigate the impact of controlled information flow.

Information literacy and transparency play a crucial role in fostering healthy and successful relationships. These two concepts are essential in enabling individuals to effectively navigate and comprehend the vast amount of information available to them, while also promoting open and honest communication within relationships. By acquiring a comprehensive understanding of how to manage the flow of information, individuals gain the ability to make well-informed decisions and establish relationships based on trust and mutual respect. This knowledge allows them to avoid becoming entangled in situations characterized by secrecy and manipulation.

LAW 8

UTILIZING THE HALO EFFECT

Law 8 explores the concept of using the Halo Effect as a strategy to shape and sway people's perceptions and opinions. When manipulators want to create a positive impression, they carefully choose specific positive qualities or achievements to emphasize. By doing this, they create an overall positive image that hides their flaws or hidden agendas. This technique is often referred to as casting a "halo" effect.

DECIPHERING THE LAW

At the core of this law lies the recognition that positive traits or accomplishments can cast a favorable glow over an individual's entire persona. Manipulators exploit this cognitive bias by emphasizing specific strengths or achievements, thereby influencing how others perceive them. This law explores the psychology of the Halo Effect, showcasing how manipulators use it to their advantage.

CASE STUDY: THE CHARMING DECEIVER

Take into account a hypothetical situation in which an individual consistently demonstrates remarkable problem-solving capabilities and exhibits strong leadership qualities. These characteristics contribute to the development of a favorable atmosphere, leading others to potentially disregard instances of manipulative conduct or ethical concerns. Through adept utilization of the Halo Effect, the individual adeptly redirects focus away from their genuine intentions.

COUNTERING THE MANIPULATION

Recognizing the manipulation of the Halo Effect is crucial to countering its influence. Individuals must cultivate a discerning eye, evaluating individuals based on a comprehensive understanding of their character rather than being swayed solely by positive traits. By engaging in critical thinking and seeking objective evaluations, they can avoid falling into the trap of overlooking manipulative behaviors.

The significance of holistic evaluation and discernment in relationships cannot be overstated. It is crucial to approach relationships with a comprehensive perspective, taking into account all relevant factors and considering the bigger picture. Holistic evaluation involves considering not only the immediate aspects of a relationship but also the long-term implications and potential consequences. This approach allows individuals to make informed decisions and judgments based on a thorough understanding of the situation at hand. Discernment By gaining a comprehensive understanding of the psychological concept known as the Halo Effect, individuals can equip themselves with the knowledge necessary to approach situations and people with a more objective and balanced perspective. This enables them to consider not only the positive qualities or attributes of a person but also take into account their behaviors and intentions. By doing so, individuals can cultivate relationships that are based on authenticity rather than superficial impressions.

LAW 9

SEEDING DOUBT AND CONFUSION

Law 9 explores a manipulation tactic that involves sowing doubt and confusion to weaken certainty and manipulate narratives. Manipulators employ a strategic approach by deliberately creating uncertainty. This tactic aims to confuse their targets, impairing their ability to make sound judgments and rendering them more vulnerable to manipulation.

UNVEILING THE LAW

At the heart of this law lies the understanding that doubt and confusion weaken decision-making and heighten vulnerability. Manipulators exploit this by subtly introducing conflicting information or narratives, creating a state of uncertainty that blurs reality. This law explores the psychology of doubt and confusion, showcasing how manipulators manipulate perceptions by fostering uncertainty.

CASE STUDY: THE DISINFORMATION ARCHITECT

Think about an illogical scenario in which an individual engages in the act of spreading false or inaccurate information during a group discussion, thereby creating uncertainty and questioning the validity of widely accepted facts. The presence of confusion provides an opportunity for the manipulator to introduce their interpretations, thereby exerting influence over the group's conclusions. Through the strategic use of doubt and confusion, the individual skillfully manipulates the narrative to suit their objectives.

COUNTERING THE MANIPULATION

Recognizing the manipulation of doubt and confusion is essential to countering its effects. Individuals must cultivate critical thinking, question information sources, and evaluate the consistency of narratives. By seeking clarity, fact-checking, and engaging in open dialogue, they can combat the erosion of certainty.

The significance of skepticism and information literacy in relationships lies in their ability to foster critical thinking and discernment. By cultivating a healthy dose of skepticism, individuals can approach information and claims with a critical eye, questioning their validity and seeking evidence to support or refute them. This skepticism helps to guard against the potential pitfalls of misinformation, manipulation, and deception that can undermine trust and communication within relationships. Furthermore, information literacy plays a crucial role By acquiring knowledge about the strategies employed to instill doubt and confusion, individuals can equip themselves with the ability to participate in well-informed discussions. This enables them to protect themselves against manipulation that often takes advantage of situations characterized by uncertainty and the spread of false information.

LAW 10

DISTORTING REALITY

Law 10 explores the strategy of distorting reality to influence how people perceive events and control the narratives surrounding them. Manipulators have a strategic approach where they distort facts and events to create a version of reality that is biased toward their own goals. This manipulation is done to influence the perspectives of the people they are targeting.

DECIPHERING THE LAW

At the core of this law lies the recognition that reality is subjective and open to interpretation. Manipulators exploit this subjectivity by deliberately altering or misrepresenting information, molding it to suit their desired narrative. This law explores the psychology of reality distortion, showcasing how manipulators manipulate perceptions through selective framing.

CASE STUDY: THE MASTER OF SPIN

In this hypothetical situation, let's consider a scenario where a public figure manipulates a sequence of events to present themselves more positively and advantageously. When people selectively emphasize specific details and leave out others, they create a version of reality that is not completely accurate, which can influence how the public perceives things. By skillfully manipulating facts and framing, they can exert control over the narrative and shape how the story is perceived.

COUNTERING THE MANIPULATION

Recognizing the manipulation of reality distortion is key to countering its influence. Individuals must cultivate critical thinking and information literacy, seeking multiple perspectives and verifying facts. By questioning inconsistencies and engaging in open dialogue, they can challenge distorted narratives and maintain a more accurate understanding of events.

PART IV
LAWS FOR MANIPULATING INTERACTIONS

LAW II

PLAYING THE GUILT CARD

Law II explores the manipulation tactic of playing the guilt card to induce feelings of guilt and obligation in others. Manipulators strategically use guilt as a tool to control behavior, fostering a sense of indebtedness that compels their targets to comply with their wishes.

UNVEILING THE LAW

At the heart of this law lies the understanding that guilt is a potent emotion that can be wielded as a form of leverage. Manipulators exploit this by creating situations or narratives that evoke guilt in their targets, pressuring them to conform to the manipulator's desires. This law delves into the psychology of guilt manipulation, showcasing how manipulators exploit empathy to their advantage.

CASE STUDY: THE EMOTIONAL MANIPULATOR

In this scenario, we have a person who frequently employs guilt-inducing statements as a means to manipulate their partner. When individuals present situations in a manner that makes their partner feel guilty, it can influence their partner to comply with their requests because they feel a strong sense of duty or responsibility. The weight of guilt is used in this emotional manipulation to effectively control the partner's behavior.

COUNTERING THE MANIPULATION

Recognizing the manipulation of playing the guilt card is crucial to countering its impact. Individuals must cultivate emotional boundaries and communicate openly about their feelings. By understanding the distinction between genuine guilt and manipulative tactics, they can engage in relationships marked by mutual respect rather than one-sided control.

LAW 12

LEVERAGING SOCIAL NORMS

Law 12 examines how manipulators utilize social norms to benefit themselves. When we consider it, society operates based on a collection of unspoken guidelines that we adhere to. Manipulators possess a high level of skill in taking advantage of these norms to advance their interests.

BREAKING IT DOWN

Ever noticed how manipulators seem to know exactly what society expects? They use this to their advantage, appealing to our desire to fit in and be accepted. Whether it's exploiting the fear of being judged or using peer pressure, manipulators can skillfully mold situations to make us act in ways that align with our goals.

CASE STUDY: THE PEER-PRESSURE PUPPETEER

Consider a hypothetical situation wherein an individual consistently employs guilt-inducing statements as a means to exert influence over their romantic partner. By employing a strategy of framing situations in a manner that triggers feelings of guilt, individuals can effectively persuade their partners to comply with their requests based on a perceived sense of duty or moral responsibility. The utilization of emotional manipulation successfully governs the partner's actions by leveraging the burden of guilt.

NAVIGATING THE TERRAIN

Recognizing the manipulation of social norms is key to navigating it. Being aware of your values and boundaries can help you resist pressure to go against your beliefs. When faced with situations where someone is using social norms to their advantage, take a step back, think about what's right for you, and don't let the pressure control your decisions.

So, in Law 12, it's all about being aware of how manipulators play on our desire to fit in. By understanding this tactic, you empower yourself to make decisions that align with your values, regardless of the pressure to conform.

LAW 13

CAPITALIZING ON RECIPROCITY

Have you ever experienced the desire to reciprocate a kind gesture when someone does something nice for you? Reciprocity is a natural human tendency that refers to the act of responding to someone's actions or gestures with a similar action or gesture. Law 13 explores how manipulators skillfully take advantage of this particular inclination to accomplish their objectives.

UNDERSTANDING THE PLAY

Picture this: Someone does you a favor, and suddenly you feel the need to repay the kindness. Manipulators know this psychology inside out. They start by doing something for you – it could be as simple as helping with a task or even just offering a compliment. Then, when they want something from you, they'll remind you of the "favor" they did, making you feel obligated to reciprocate.

CASE STUDY: THE FAVOR BANKER

Consider a scenario wherein a colleague consistently assumes responsibility for your assigned shifts or assists in managing your workload without any explicit request from your end. When individuals require reciprocation, they employ the strategy of leveraging the various "acts of kindness" they have performed on your behalf. This scenario creates a sense of indebtedness, increasing the likelihood of compliance with their request.

NAVIGATING THE TERRAIN

Recognizing when reciprocity is being used as a manipulation tactic is key. Remember, you're not bound to fulfill every favor just because someone did something nice for you. Take a step back, assess the situation, and decide if you genuinely want to help, rather than feeling compelled by an unspoken social contract.

LAW 14

USING FLATTERY AS A WEAPON

Flattery is a skillful way of giving praise and compliments to others. It is often used to create a positive and harmonious atmosphere in social interactions, boosting people's moods and fostering stronger connections between individuals. Law 14 is a principle that reveals how flattery can be used as a tactic to manipulate and influence situations to achieve desired results.

UNVEILING THE MANIPULATION

Manipulators understand that flattery is a potent tool for opening doors and softening defenses. They employ flattery strategically, using compliments to create a positive emotional connection and gain the target's trust. This connection then becomes the foundation for steering the target toward their desired goals.

CASE STUDY: THE PRAISE PUPPETEER

Consider a scenario where you find yourself attending a social gathering and an individual approaches you, expressing admiration and compliments towards you. The individuals provide positive feedback regarding your physical appearance, cognitive abilities, and achievements, thereby instilling a sense of worth and recognition within you. During the ongoing conversation, the individual adeptly introduces a subject matter intending to seek concurrence, leveraging the positive rapport established through complimentary remarks to enhance the likelihood of acquiescence.

NAVIGATING THE TERRAIN

Recognizing manipulative flattery requires a discerning approach. While genuine compliments can foster positive interactions, it's essential to consider the context. When flattery is used to advance an agenda, take a step back and critically evaluate the situation. Is the flattery being used to build genuine rapport, or is it a calculated maneuver to influence your decisions?

The dual nature of flattery enables individuals to recognize and value authentic compliments, while also remaining cautious of flattery used manipulatively. By developing an awareness of the underlying motives behind compliments, individuals can effectively manage their social interactions by maintaining a well-rounded viewpoint. This approach guarantees that their choices remain genuine and driven by their desires.

LAW 15

INSTIGATING COMPETITION

Have you ever experienced a strong sense of motivation when you find yourself in a competitive setting? "The Law" explores a manipulative strategy known as instigating competition. This tactic involves manipulators intentionally creating rivalries between individuals to motivate them to achieve certain goals or objectives.

PEELING BACK THE LAYERS

Competition can be a powerful motivator, pushing us to strive for excellence. Manipulators, however, take advantage of this by strategically inciting competition among individuals. They pit people against each other, creating an environment where the desire to outperform others blinds us to their ulterior motives.

CASE STUDY: THE PUPPETEER OF RIVALRY

In a hypothetical workplace scenario, a manager employs a subtle approach to acknowledge and commend the accomplishments of one employee to another employee. The act of engaging in this straightforward action initiates the establishment of a competitive mindset, as the subsequent employee becomes motivated to demonstrate their capabilities. The manipulator derives advantages from heightened productivity and dedication, while simultaneously exerting control through the stimulation of competition.

NAVIGATING THE TERRAIN

The ability to identify and acknowledge the manipulation of deliberately provoked competition is crucial in maintaining genuine relationships. Although healthy competition can stimulate growth, it is important to exercise caution when encountering situations where rivalry appears to be artificially created. In situations where competition arises due to external factors rather than intrinsic motivation, it is advisable to pause and evaluate if the prevailing circumstances align with your authentic objectives.

PART V
LAWS FOR MAINTAINING CONTROL

LAW 16

ESTABLISHING EMOTIONAL DEBT

Have you ever experienced a situation where someone did you a favor and as a result, you felt a sense of obligation to reciprocate their kindness? "This Law" explores a manipulation tactic known as establishing emotional debt. This tactic involves manipulators creating a feeling of indebtedness by offering help or support to us. By doing so, they increase the likelihood that we will be more willing to comply with their future requests.

GETTING TO THE CORE

Emotional debt is like an unspoken IOU — when someone does something kind for us, we feel a natural inclination to reciprocate. Manipulators recognize this tendency and use it to their advantage. By offering assistance or support, they create a psychological balance that makes us more inclined to fulfill their future wishes.

CASE STUDY: THE EMOTIONAL ACCOUNTANT

Consider a companion who consistently offers guidance, assistance, and attentive receptiveness to your needs. When individuals require assistance, they often employ a strategy of recalling and highlighting the various acts of kindness they have previously extended toward you. The establishment of an emotional debt can create difficulties in refusing a request, as one may experience a sense of obligation to reciprocate their benevolence.

NAVIGATING THE TERRAIN

The ability to identify and acknowledge emotional debt manipulation is essential for establishing and preserving healthy boundaries. When faced with the opportunity to reciprocate kindness, it is important to take into account the surrounding context. Is your willingness to assist driven by genuine inclination or a sense of obligation stemming from emotional debt? Engaging in introspection and evaluating one's emotions can facilitate the process of making decisions that are under one's genuine intentions.

LAW 17

EMPLOYING ISOLATION TACTICS

Manipulators often employ a tactic of isolating individuals from their social circles, have you ever observed this? "The Law" explores the concept of manipulation known as isolation. This tactic involves manipulators intentionally creating a sense of separation between individuals and their support systems. By doing so, manipulators aim to gain control over their targets.

UNMASKING THE MANIPULATION

Manipulators can effectively utilize isolation as a powerful tool. Manipulators employ a strategy of isolating individuals from their social circle, including friends, family, and other sources of support. This deliberate separation serves to undermine the target's ability to maintain a balanced perspective and independence. When individuals are isolated, they become more susceptible to being influenced and controlled by manipulators.

CASE STUDY: THE ISOLATION ARCHITECT

Take into account an improbable scenario in which an individual adept at manipulation successfully persuades another person to create distance between themselves and their friends. This is achieved by strategically sowing seeds of doubt regarding the loyalty of said friends. As the level of isolation experienced by the target intensifies, their dependence on the manipulator for companionship and guidance grows. The state of isolation provides the manipulator with increased authority over the individual's choices and behaviors.

NAVIGATING THE TERRAIN

The recognition of the manipulation of isolation is crucial for safeguarding one's autonomy. Healthy relationships are characterized by the presence of open communication and the sharing of experiences. When faced with an attempt to isolate you from your support network, it is important to analyze the underlying motives behind such behavior. It is advisable to establish and sustain relationships with reliable acquaintances and relatives who can provide diverse viewpoints and help maintain your sense of stability.

Gaining a comprehensive understanding of isolation tactics enables individuals to effectively identify instances where others may seek to exert control by deliberately isolating them from their support networks. By maintaining genuine connections and cultivating a robust sense of independence, individuals can effectively navigate social interactions with a clear perspective, ensuring that their decisions are firmly rooted in their values and desires.

LAW 18

PROMOTING FEAR AND ANXIETY

Fear and anxiety, being strong emotions, can affect our judgment and make us more vulnerable to manipulation. "The Law" delves into using fear and anxiety as a manipulative tactic. Manipulators employ these emotions to gain control over individuals and influence their choices.

GETTING TO THE HEART OF IT

Manipulators understand that fear and anxiety can be paralyzing, causing us to seek safety and reassurance. They play on these emotions by highlighting potential threats or dangers, making individuals feel vulnerable. This heightened state of anxiety can make us more likely to comply with their directives to regain a sense of security.

CASE STUDY: THE FEAR INSTIGATOR

Consider a hypothetical situation wherein an individual consistently employs manipulative tactics by consistently highlighting worst-case scenarios and potential hazards that could potentially jeopardize the well-being of another person. Through the continuous instillation of fear and anxiety, a perception of reliance on their guidance for safety is cultivated. The manipulator is bestowed with substantial control over the decisions of the individual.

NAVIGATING THE TERRAIN

Recognizing the manipulation of fear and anxiety is essential for maintaining emotional well-being. When someone consistently focuses on negative possibilities or raises an alarm without providing reasonable solutions, it's a red flag. Seek balance by considering multiple perspectives and evaluating potential threats rationally.

In Law 18, understanding how fear and anxiety can be used as tools of manipulation empowers you to take charge of your emotional responses. By addressing concerns with a clear head, seeking balanced information, and maintaining a support network, you can make decisions that are not driven solely by fear, but rather by a comprehensive evaluation of the situation at hand.

LAW 19

EXPLOITING LOYALTY AND TRUST

Loyalty and trust are essential for building strong relationships. However, manipulators are skilled at taking advantage of these virtues for their benefit. The concept of "The Law" delves into the strategy of using loyalty and trust to manipulate others. It focuses on how individuals can be influenced by their dedication and belief in someone else.

PEELING BACK THE LAYERS

Manipulators often target individuals who are deeply loyal or trusting. They create a sense of emotional connection, making these individuals more willing to comply with their requests. By capitalizing on the trust and loyalty they've cultivated, manipulators can steer others toward actions that may not align with their best interests.

CASE STUDY: THE TRUSTWORTHY DECEIVER

Consider a hypothetical situation in which a close acquaintance consistently provides you with unwavering assurances regarding their integrity and dependability. Subsequently, they make a request that contradicts your sound judgment. Due to the presence of trust, individuals may exhibit a higher propensity to acquiesce, even in cases where the solicitation appears unconventional. The manipulator has successfully leveraged your trust for their benefit.

NAVIGATING THE TERRAIN

Recognizing the manipulation of loyalty and trust is crucial for safeguarding your best interests. While trust and loyalty are valuable, it's important to evaluate situations objectively. If someone is consistently leveraging your trust to gain compliance without considering your needs, it's time to reevaluate the relationship dynamics.

In Law 19, understanding how manipulators exploit loyalty and trust empowers you to protect your well-being. By cultivating healthy skepticism, seeking diverse perspectives, and maintaining a balance between trust and discernment, you can engage in relationships that are built on genuine loyalty and trust, rather than manipulation.

LAW 20

MANIPULATING THROUGH WITHHOLDING

Law 20 explores a manipulative strategy known as withholding, which involves using silence or inaction as a means to exert control over situations and manipulate others. Manipulators can create a sense of uncertainty and dependency by strategically withholding information, emotions, or actions.

UNVEILING THE MANIPULATION

Withholding is a form of control that hinges on the idea that information is power. Manipulators capitalize on this by keeping individuals in the dark or creating a sense of anticipation. This uncertainty often compels people to seek validation, information, or action from the manipulator, inadvertently giving them influence over decisions.

CASE STUDY: THE INFORMATION GATEKEEPER

Consider a hypothetical scenario where a colleague possesses vital project-related information but intentionally withholds it, thereby fostering a sense of urgency and dependence on their expertise. As individuals encounter difficulties in progressing without access to this information, they seek guidance from the manipulator, inadvertently bestowing upon them authority over the project's trajectory.

NAVIGATING THE TERRAIN

Recognizing the manipulation of withholding is vital for maintaining autonomy. When someone consistently holds back information, emotions, or actions to maintain control, it's important to question their motives. Seek open communication, and transparency, and ensure that you're not allowing yourself to become overly reliant on someone who uses withholding as a power play.

In Law 20, understanding how manipulators use withholding as a tactic empowers you to navigate relationships with a discerning approach. By valuing transparency, open communication, and actively seeking information from multiple sources, you can avoid falling into the trap of dependency and manipulation.

PART VI
LAWS FOR ESCALATING INFLUENCE

LAW 21

LEVERAGING EMOTIONAL BLACKMAIL

Law 21 explores a manipulative strategy known as emotional blackmail. This tactic involves individuals using powerful emotions like guilt, fear, or other intense feelings to manipulate others into doing what they want. When someone engages in emotional blackmail, they use tactics that make the recipient feel obligated to comply with their requests. This can be challenging to resist because it creates a strong sense of obligation within the person being manipulated.

GETTING TO THE CORE

Emotional blackmail operates on the principle of using someone's emotions against them. Manipulators tap into the vulnerabilities of their targets, triggering feelings of guilt, fear, or shame. This emotional manipulation coerces individuals into doing what the manipulator wants, often against their own better judgment.

CASE STUDY: THE GUILT TRIP MASTER

Consider a hypothetical scenario wherein a family member persistently engages in the act of reminding you about their past contributions towards your well-being, thereby employing guilt as a means to coerce you into undertaking tasks or actions that may not align with your personal preferences or desires. The individual may express, "Considering all the sacrifices I have made on your behalf, would it not be feasible for you to fulfill this single request for me?" The act of manipulation employed in this situation presents challenges in refusing, as it induces a sense of indebtedness.

NAVIGATING THE TERRAIN

Recognizing the manipulation of emotional blackmail is crucial for maintaining emotional well-being. When someone consistently uses guilt, fear, or other intense emotions to control their decisions, it's important to step back and evaluate the situation. Set healthy boundaries, communicate openly, and don't allow yourself to be manipulated through emotional pressure.

In Law 21, understanding how manipulators use emotional blackmail empowers you to protect your autonomy and emotional health. By valuing your feelings and making decisions based on your true desires, rather than succumbing to emotional manipulation, you can navigate relationships with authenticity and emotional resilience.

LAW 22

INSTILLING A SENSE OF OBLIGATION

Law 22 explores the strategy of creating a feeling of duty or obligation to manipulate others. Manipulators employ tactics that create a situation where people feel obligated to comply with their requests or demands, making it challenging for individuals to say no.

UNVEILING THE MANIPULATION

Manipulators understand that when we feel obligated to someone, we're more likely to comply with their wishes. They might do favors, provide help, or offer support, creating a psychological debt. This debt can make us more susceptible to their influence, as we feel compelled to repay their kindness.

CASE STUDY: THE GIFT GIVER'S GAMBIT

Consider a hypothetical situation in which an acquaintance consistently bestows gifts upon you and performs acts of kindness without your prompt or request. When the individual eventually requests a favor in reciprocation, it is possible to experience a sense of indebtedness, rendering it challenging to decline. The manipulator has effectively induced a feeling of duty.

NAVIGATING THE TERRAIN

Recognizing the manipulation of instilling a sense of obligation is vital for maintaining personal agency. While reciprocity is a natural part of relationships, it's important to assess whether the favors are genuinely given or if they come with strings attached. Make decisions based on your true desires rather than a sense of obligation.

In Law 22, understanding how manipulators use a sense of obligation empowers you to navigate relationships with clarity. By differentiating between genuine reciprocity and manipulation, you can make choices that align with your values and desires, rather than succumbing to external pressures.

LAW 23

CREATING AN ECHO CHAMBER

Law 23 explores the concept of creating an echo chamber, which is a manipulative tactic. Manipulators often create a specific environment that supports their own beliefs by surrounding themselves with people who share similar opinions and ideas. They tend to avoid individuals who have differing viewpoints, effectively shutting out any dissenting opinions. This controlled environment helps them maintain their own beliefs and reinforces their manipulative behavior.

UNMASKING THE MANIPULATION

Manipulators understand that exposure to differing viewpoints can challenge their control over individuals. By creating an echo chamber, they surround themselves with people who share their opinions, validating their beliefs and making it difficult for others to present alternative perspectives.

CASE STUDY: THE OPINION ENCLAVE

Consider a hypothetical scenario wherein an individual, referred to as the manipulator, establishes a social circle comprising like-minded acquaintances and colleagues who share similar perspectives and opinions. The practice of discouraging dissenting opinions is prevalent, with such viewpoints often being categorized as "negative" or "uninformed." This practice strengthens their authority by guaranteeing that their ideas remain unchallenged.

NAVIGATING THE TERRAIN

Recognizing the manipulation of creating an echo chamber is vital for fostering critical thinking and open dialogue. When you notice a consistent avoidance of diverse viewpoints or a dismissal of dissent, it's a sign that an echo chamber might be at play. Seek out diverse perspectives and engage in respectful debates to ensure a well-rounded understanding.

In Law 23, understanding how manipulators create echo chambers empowers you to engage in independent thinking and healthy discourse. By actively seeking diverse viewpoints and valuing open dialogue, you can navigate relationships with an informed perspective, safeguarding against manipulation that thrives in closed-off environments.

LAW 24

USING EMOTIONAL ESCALATION

Law 24 explores the strategy of emotional escalation, which involves manipulating others by intensifying their emotions. Manipulators have a tendency to intensify emotions, which leads to strong reactions that can hinder people from thinking logically and responding calmly.

PEELING BACK THE LAYERS

Manipulators understand that heightened emotions can cloud judgment and lead to impulsive decisions. By escalating emotions, they create a chaotic environment that makes it challenging for individuals to maintain their composure and make well-reasoned choices.

CASE STUDY: THE EMOTIONAL AGITATOR

Picture a mischievous puppet master who gleefully pokes the emotional bear during a lively debate. Oh boy, when things get heated, they might just crank up the volume, unleash a fiery vocabulary, or even go for the good ol' personal attack. It's like a recipe for a spicy argument! Oh boy, here comes the emotional rollercoaster! Get ready for some serious distraction action as this wild ride takes us away from the actual issues. Logic? Who needs logic when we can have a dramatic meltdown instead? Buckle up, folks!

NAVIGATING THE TERRAIN

Recognizing the manipulation of emotional escalation is key to maintaining emotional balance. When someone deliberately escalates emotions to distract or control a situation, take a step back. Refuse to engage in a heated exchange and prioritize calm and rational communication.

In Law 24, understanding how manipulators use emotional escalation empowers you to remain composed and focused in challenging situations. By refusing to be drawn into emotional turmoil, you can navigate relationships with clarity and ensure that your decisions are guided by reason rather than impulsive reactions.

LAW 25

ORCHESTRATING PUBLIC DISPLAYS

Law 25 explores the strategy of orchestrating public displays as a manipulative tactic. Manipulators are individuals who strategically create specific situations in public places to elicit sympathy, support, or control from others.

UNVEILING THE MANIPULATION

Manipulators understand the power of perception. By orchestrating public displays, they present themselves in a specific light to evoke a desired response from others. These displays can range from emotional breakdowns to heroic acts, all to influence the reactions and opinions of those witnessing the scene.

CASE STUDY: THE PUBLIC PERFORMANCE

Consider a manipulator who, in the presence of a group, expresses hurt feelings or victimization dramatically. This well-planned display elicits sympathy and attention from others, creating an environment in which those around them are more likely to agree with them.

NAVIGATING THE TERRAIN

Recognizing the manipulation of orchestrating public displays is essential for maintaining clear judgment. When someone repeatedly uses public scenes to control perceptions, take a step back and evaluate the authenticity of the display. Don't be swayed solely by emotional displays – seek a comprehensive understanding of the situation.

In Law 25, understanding how manipulators orchestrate public displays empowers you to engage with a discerning perspective. By evaluating actions and behaviors in a broader context, you can make decisions that are grounded in an authentic understanding of the situation, rather than being swayed by calculated public performances.

PART VII
LAWS FOR CONCEALING INTENTIONS

LAW 26

PROJECTING FALSE EMPATHY

In this exploration, we are examining a manipulative tactic known as projecting false empathy. Manipulators often pretend to be empathetic and understanding to establish an emotional bond with others, but their true intention is to further their interests or goals.

PEELING BACK THE LAYERS

Manipulators recognize the power of empathy in building relationships and gaining trust. By projecting false empathy, they mimic genuine concern to establish a sense of closeness. This emotional connection can blind individuals to the manipulator's ulterior motives.

CASE STUDY: THE EMPATHETIC IMPOSTOR

Someone who consistently offers support and understanding when you share your concerns. They seem genuinely empathetic, but their responses always steer the conversation toward their interests. They're projecting false empathy to establish a connection while subtly advancing their agenda.

NAVIGATING THE TERRAIN

Recognizing the manipulation of false empathy is vital for maintaining genuine relationships. When someone consistently appears empathetic while subtly pushing their agenda, it's crucial to consider whether their concern is authentic. Engage in conversations with people who show genuine interest in your well-being and who respect your own goals.

In Law 26, understanding how manipulators project false empathy empowers you to engage in relationships with a discerning perspective. By valuing authentic connections and healthy boundaries, you can navigate interactions that are built on genuine understanding, rather than being swayed by manipulative displays of empathy.

LAW 27

ESTABLISHING A FALSE BOND

Law 27 explores the concept of using a manipulative strategy known as establishing a false bond. Manipulators are individuals who use various tactics to create a false sense of connection and closeness with others. They often imitate genuine relationships to gain trust and exert control over their victims.

UNMASKING THE MANIPULATION

Manipulators understand that bonds of trust and friendship are powerful tools. By establishing a false bond, they simulate the dynamics of genuine connections, often sharing personal details and vulnerabilities to create a sense of intimacy. This illusion of closeness can make individuals more inclined to comply with the manipulator's wishes.

CASE STUDY: THE FAUX FRIEND

Someone who enters your life, quickly sharing personal stories and experiences, making you feel like you've found a kindred spirit. However, over time, you realize that this person only seems interested when they need something from you. They've established a false bond to create the illusion of a deep connection.

NAVIGATING THE TERRAIN

Recognizing the manipulation of a false bond is vital for protecting your well-being. When someone consistently exhibits intimate behaviors while only engaging for their benefit, it's important to reassess the authenticity of the connection. Value relationships that are based on mutual respect, shared values, and genuine care.

In Law 27, understanding how manipulators establish false bonds empowers you to engage in relationships with a discerning perspective. By nurturing connections that are rooted in authenticity and mutual support, you can navigate interactions that are built on genuine trust, rather than being swayed by the allure of superficial intimacy.

LAW 28

FEIGNING OPENNESS AND HONESTY

Law 28 explores the strategy of pretending to be open and honest to manipulate others. Manipulators often adopt a deceptive approach by appearing honest and open, which gives the impression that they can be trusted. However, behind this facade, they hide their real motives and intentions.

PEELING BACK THE LAYERS

Manipulators recognize that trust is built on honesty and transparency. By feigning openness and honesty, they mimic genuine vulnerability and share seemingly personal details to create an illusion of trust. This calculated facade can make individuals more likely to confide in them and let their guard down.

CASE STUDY: THE DECEPTIVE CONFIDANT

Someone who appears open and candid about their own life, sharing stories of their struggles and challenges. However, as you spend more time with them, you realize that they only reveal information that serves their agenda. They've feigned openness and honesty to establish a facade of trustworthiness.

NAVIGATING THE TERRAIN

Recognizing the manipulation of feigned openness and honesty is crucial for maintaining genuine relationships. When someone consistently portrays themselves as transparent while withholding information or using their disclosures to further their own goals, it's important to assess whether their actions align with their words. Value relationships that are based on authentic communication and mutual respect.

In Law 28, understanding how manipulators feign openness and honesty empowers you to engage in relationships with discernment. By valuing genuine transparency and fostering connections based on mutual trust, you can navigate interactions that are grounded in authenticity, rather than being swayed by the veneer of false openness.

LAW 29

CAMOUFLAGING MANIPULATION

Law 29 explores the concept of camouflaging manipulation, which involves using tactics to hide or disguise one's manipulative intentions. Manipulators often employ tactics such as appearing innocent, charming, or concerned to conceal their true intentions. This can make it challenging to identify their underlying motives.

UNVEILING THE MANIPULATION

Manipulators understand that overt manipulation is more likely to be resisted. By camouflaging their intentions, they create a facade that appears harmless or even beneficial. This veneer of innocence makes it challenging for individuals to recognize the manipulation until it's too late.

CASE STUDY: THE CHARMING CHARLATAN

Imagine someone who always seems eager to help and goes out of their way to assist others. However, as time goes on, you realize that their "help" consistently aligns with their agenda. They've camouflaged their manipulation by presenting their actions as altruistic, making it difficult to discern their true motives.

NAVIGATING THE TERRAIN

Recognizing the manipulation of camouflaging is essential for safeguarding your interests. When someone consistently presents their actions as benign while pursuing their own goals, it's important to look beyond the surface and consider the potential implications. Value relationships that are built on mutual respect, transparency, and shared goals.

In Law 29, understanding how manipulators camouflage their actions empowers you to engage in relationships with discernment. By recognizing red flags and seeking authenticity in interactions, you can navigate relationships that are grounded in clear understanding, rather than being deceived by the facade of innocence.

LAW 30

MASKING MOTIVES

Law 30 explores the concept of masking motives, which involves the use of manipulative tactics. Manipulators are individuals who conceal their true intentions by creating a well-crafted mask, which makes it difficult to understand their underlying motives.

PEELING BACK THE LAYERS

Manipulators understand that revealing their true motives can lead to resistance or suspicion. By masking their intentions, they create a misleading image that appears aligned with the interests of others. This calculated act makes it difficult for individuals to see beyond the surface and understand the manipulator's true agenda.

CASE STUDY: THE MASTER ILLUSIONIST

Imagine someone who consistently presents their actions as selfless and in the best interest of everyone involved. However, as time goes on, you start to notice that their actions consistently lead to outcomes that benefit them alone. They've mastered the art of masking motives, creating an illusion of alignment with others' interests.

NAVIGATING THE TERRAIN

Recognizing the manipulation of masking motives is crucial for maintaining clarity in relationships. When someone consistently presents their intentions in a way that seems beneficial while serving their agenda, it's important to dig deeper and evaluate the broader implications. Value relationships that are based on open communication, shared goals, and mutual respect.

In Law 30, understanding how manipulators mask their motives empowers you to engage in relationships with discernment. By peeling back the layers and seeking authentic alignment, you can navigate interactions that are grounded in transparency and genuine intent, rather than being led astray by the manipulator's facade.

PART VIII

LAWS FOR NAVIGATING RESISTANCE

LAW 31

NEUTRALIZING OPPOSITION

Law 31 explores the strategy of neutralizing opposition, which involves manipulating others to diminish their resistance or counter their influence. Manipulators employ strategic tactics to weaken or remove any sources of opposition to retain control and exert influence over others.

UNVEILING THE MANIPULATION

Manipulators recognize that opposition can threaten their power and influence. By neutralizing opposition, they employ tactics to weaken dissenting voices, often through discrediting, isolating, or silencing those who challenge their authority. This ensures that their perspective remains dominant.

CASE STUDY: THE DISSENT DISMANTLER

Imagine a manipulator who consistently undermines anyone who voices a differing opinion. They might use tactics like spreading rumors, belittling others' ideas, or isolating individuals who challenge them. Their goal is to neutralize opposition and ensure that their viewpoint remains unchallenged.

NAVIGATING THE TERRAIN

Recognizing the manipulation of neutralizing opposition is vital for fostering healthy discourse and diverse perspectives. When someone consistently employs tactics to suppress opposing viewpoints, it's important to question the motives behind these actions. Value relationships that encourage open dialogue, mutual respect, and the freedom to express differing opinions.

In Law 31, understanding how manipulators neutralize opposition empowers you to engage in relationships with an open mind. By valuing diverse perspectives and seeking environments that encourage constructive debate, you can navigate interactions that are grounded in genuine understanding and collaboration, rather than being stifled by manipulative efforts to maintain control.

LAW 32

EMPLOYING GASLIGHTING TECHNIQUES

Law 32 delves into the subject of employing gaslighting techniques, which are manipulative tactics used to deceive and confuse others. Psychological manipulation is a technique employed by manipulators to alter reality in a way that makes individuals question their perceptions, memories, and even their sanity.

PEELING BACK THE LAYERS

Manipulators understand that by sowing seeds of doubt, they can control and undermine their targets' confidence. Through gaslighting techniques, they invalidate others' experiences, often making them question their reality. This leaves individuals more vulnerable to the manipulator's influence.

CASE STUDY: THE REALITY DISTORTER

Imagine a manipulator who consistently denies saying or doing things, despite clear evidence to the contrary. They might accuse you of being forgetful or overly sensitive, causing you to doubt your memory. This gaslighting technique shifts the blame and control in their favor.

NAVIGATING THE TERRAIN

Recognizing the manipulation of gaslighting techniques is crucial for maintaining your emotional well-being. When someone consistently distorts reality and causes you to doubt your perceptions, it's important to seek clarity and external validation. Value relationships that respect your experiences and encourage open communication.

In Law 32, understanding how manipulators employ gaslighting techniques empowers you to maintain your self-confidence and clarity. By seeking outside perspectives, keeping records, and trusting your instincts, you can navigate relationships with a strong sense of self-awareness and guard against manipulative efforts to undermine your reality.

LAW 33

MINIMIZING THE PERCEPTION OF MANIPULATION

Law 33 explores the strategy of downplaying the appearance of manipulation. Manipulators use various tactics to minimize the significance of their actions, which can make it difficult for people to identify their behaviors as manipulative.

UNMASKING THE MANIPULATION

Manipulators understand that if their actions are perceived as manipulation, their influence can wane. By minimizing the perception of manipulation, they create doubt and confusion, often presenting their actions as harmless or well-intentioned. This calculated approach makes it difficult for individuals to accurately identify their behavior as manipulative.

CASE STUDY: THE DECEPTIVE SCHEMER

Imagine a manipulator who consistently downplays their actions, framing them as simple mistakes or misunderstandings. They might say, "I didn't mean to upset you, I was just trying to help." By presenting their behavior as well-intentioned, they cast doubt on your assessment of their actions.

NAVIGATING THE TERRAIN

Recognizing the manipulation or minimizing the perception of manipulation is essential for maintaining clear judgment. When someone consistently presents their actions as innocuous while pursuing their agenda, it's important to evaluate the larger context and their motivations. Value relationships that encourage open communication, transparency, and respect for individual boundaries.

In Law 33, understanding how manipulators minimize the perception of their actions empowers you to engage in relationships with discernment. By staying attuned to your instincts, seeking validation from trusted sources, and maintaining open dialogue, you can navigate interactions with a clear understanding of the dynamics at play, rather than being misled by manipulative attempts to minimize the perception of their actions.

LAW 34

UTILIZING DIVERSIONARY TACTICS

Law 34 explores the concept of using diversionary tactics as a manipulative strategy. When manipulators want to hide their actions or intentions, they use tactics to shift people's attention away from what they're doing. This often causes individuals to concentrate on less important things instead of the main issue.

PEELING BACK THE LAYERS

Manipulators recognize that shifting focus can help them avoid scrutiny and accountability. By utilizing diversionary tactics, they redirect attention to tangential topics or create distractions, making it difficult for others to address the actual issues at hand.

CASE STUDY: THE MASTER OF MISDIRECTION

Imagine a manipulator who consistently changes the topic or introduces unrelated issues whenever their actions are questioned. By creating confusion and directing attention elsewhere, they avoid addressing the core matter. This diversionary tactic prevents others from addressing their actual intentions.

NAVIGATING THE TERRAIN

Recognizing the manipulation of diversionary tactics is essential for maintaining effective communication and problem-solving. When someone consistently sidetracks discussions or introduces unrelated issues, it's important to steer the conversation back to the core matter. Value relationships that encourage open dialogue and the ability to address issues directly.

In Law 34, understanding how manipulators utilize diversionary tactics empowers you to engage in relationships with a focus on clear communication. By staying grounded in addressing core issues and not being swayed by distractions, you can navigate interactions that are driven by meaningful discussions rather than manipulated diversions.

LAW 35

NORMALIZING MANIPULATIVE BEHAVIOR

In Law 35, we're exploring the manipulative tactic of normalizing manipulative behavior. Manipulators create an environment where their actions are accepted as commonplace, making it challenging for individuals to recognize the manipulation.

UNVEILING THE MANIPULATION

Manipulators understand that if their behavior is seen as normal, it's less likely to be questioned. By normalizing manipulative behavior, they gradually introduce and reinforce actions that align with their agenda. Over time, individuals become desensitized to these actions, making it difficult to recognize them as manipulative.

CASE STUDY: THE CONDITIONING MASTERMIND

Imagine a manipulator who consistently employs subtle tactics to manipulate situations and people. Through consistent exposure, their actions become ingrained in the environment. Slowly, these behaviors become accepted as part of the norm, making it challenging for others to recognize the manipulation.

NAVIGATING THE TERRAIN

Recognizing the manipulation of normalizing behavior is essential for maintaining a healthy environment. When someone consistently introduces manipulative actions as common practice, it's important to assess whether these actions align with your values and boundaries. Value relationships that uphold honesty, transparency, and mutual respect.

In Law 35, understanding how manipulators normalize their behavior empowers you to engage in relationships with a discerning perspective. By maintaining a strong sense of your values and boundaries, you can navigate interactions that are grounded in authenticity and mutual understanding, rather than being influenced by manipulative attempts to reshape your perception of what is considered normal.

PART IX

LAWS FOR LONG-TERM DOMINATION

LAW 36

CREATING EMOTIONAL ADDICTION

Law 36 explores the concept of creating emotional addiction as a manipulative tactic. Manipulators engage in behaviors that encourage emotional dependence on others. This means they create a situation where individuals feel the need to rely on them for validation, comfort, and a sense of worth.

UNMASKING THE MANIPULATION

Manipulators understand that emotional dependency can be a powerful tool. By creating emotional addiction, they provide intermittent moments of support, validation, or kindness, creating an emotional rollercoaster that keeps individuals craving their attention and approval.

CASE STUDY: THE EMOTIONAL PUPPETEER

Imagine a manipulator who alternates between moments of intense emotional closeness and periods of withdrawal. They provide comfort and validation when you're vulnerable, creating a sense of addiction to their support. This emotional cycle keeps you seeking their validation and approval.

NAVIGATING THE TERRAIN

Recognizing the manipulation of emotional addiction is crucial for maintaining emotional independence. When someone consistently provides support or validation in a way that keeps you emotionally dependent, it's important to reassess the dynamics of the relationship. Value connections that respect your autonomy and provide consistent support.

In Law 36, understanding how manipulators create emotional addiction empowers you to engage in relationships with a sense of self-awareness. By nurturing your emotional well-being, seeking support from diverse sources, and maintaining emotional independence, you can navigate interactions with clarity and ensure that your emotions are not manipulated for someone else's benefit.

LAW 37

CONDITIONING THROUGH REINFORCEMENT

Law 37 delves into the concept of conditioning through reinforcement, which is a manipulative tactic. Manipulators employ a strategy of using rewards and punishments to influence and mold behavior, essentially conditioning individuals to conform to their wishes and intentions.

PEELING BACK THE LAYERS

Manipulators understand that behavior can be influenced through reinforcement. By conditioning through reinforcement, they use rewards or punishments to elicit specific responses from others. This gradual shaping of behavior makes individuals more likely to comply with the manipulator's wishes.

CASE STUDY: THE BEHAVIOR SHAPER

Imagine a manipulator who consistently rewards compliant behavior with praise, attention, or favors, while withdrawing support or affection when their desires are not met. This creates a conditioning process where individuals are more likely to align their actions with the manipulator's expectations.

NAVIGATING THE TERRAIN

Recognizing the manipulation of conditioning through reinforcement is crucial for maintaining autonomy. When someone consistently uses rewards and punishments to shape your behavior, it's important to evaluate whether your actions align with your values and desires. Value relationships that encourage authentic expression and respect for your own choices.

In Law 37, understanding how manipulators use conditioning through reinforcement empowers you to engage in relationships with self-awareness. By staying attuned to your values, making decisions that align with your genuine desires, and valuing relationships that respect your autonomy, you can navigate interactions that are based on your terms, rather than being shaped by manipulative tactics.

LAW 38

CULTIVATING LEARNED HELPLESSNESS

In Law 38, we're delving into the manipulative tactic of cultivating learned helplessness. Manipulators create an environment where individuals believe they are powerless and incapable of changing their circumstances, making them more dependent on the manipulator's guidance.

UNVEILING THE MANIPULATION

Manipulators understand that by fostering a sense of helplessness, they can gain control over individuals' decisions and actions. Through constant criticism, belittling, or thwarting of independent efforts, they create an environment where individuals feel incapable of taking control of their own lives.

CASE STUDY: THE SELF-ESTEEM SABOTEUR

Imagine a manipulator who consistently criticizes your ideas and efforts, making you believe that your actions are futile. Over time, you start to doubt your abilities and feel dependent on their guidance. This cultivated learned helplessness keeps you seeking their validation and direction.

NAVIGATING THE TERRAIN

It is important to be able to identify and understand the tactics used to create a sense of learned helplessness to protect your self-esteem and sense of control over your own life. When you encounter someone who consistently undermines your abilities and makes you feel powerless, it is crucial to question those beliefs and actively seek out environments that promote personal growth and boost your self-confidence.

In Law 38, understanding how manipulators cultivate learned helplessness empowers you to engage in relationships with a strong sense of self-worth. By valuing your abilities, seeking environments that support your growth, and surrounding yourself with people who uplift and encourage you, you can navigate interactions that are grounded in your strength, rather than being influenced by manipulative tactics aimed at fostering learned helplessness.

LAW 39

GENERATING COGNITIVE DISSONANCE

Law 39 delves into the concept of generating cognitive dissonance as a manipulative tactic. When manipulators want to control someone, they intentionally create situations where the person's thoughts or beliefs contradict each other. This causes the person to feel psychological discomfort, which makes them more susceptible to being influenced by the manipulator.

PEELING BACK THE LAYERS

Manipulators understand that inconsistency between beliefs and actions can lead to discomfort. By generating cognitive dissonance, they present conflicting information or challenge individuals' existing beliefs, creating a state of internal conflict. This discomfort makes individuals more susceptible to adopting the manipulator's perspective.

CASE STUDY: THE BELIEF BENDER

Imagine a manipulator who presents arguments or information that contradicts your existing beliefs or experiences. They might challenge your convictions, creating a sense of confusion and doubt. This generated cognitive dissonance makes you more likely to entertain their viewpoint to reduce the discomfort.

NAVIGATING THE TERRAIN

Recognizing the manipulation of generating cognitive dissonance is essential for maintaining clarity of thought. When someone consistently presents conflicting information or challenges your beliefs without providing solid evidence, it's important to evaluate their motives. Value relationships that encourage critical thinking, open discussion, and respect for individual perspectives.

In Law 39, understanding how manipulators generate cognitive dissonance empowers you to engage in relationships with discernment. By staying grounded in your values, seeking reliable information, and engaging in thoughtful conversations, you can navigate interactions that are based on a well-rounded understanding of the situation, rather than being swayed by manipulative attempts to create internal conflict.

LAW 40

SECURING EMOTIONAL SUPREMACY

Law 40 explores the strategy of gaining emotional control and dominance. Manipulators have a goal of making themselves the main provider of emotional support for others. They do this by making individuals rely heavily on their validation, guidance, and approval.

UNVEILING THE MANIPULATION

Manipulators understand that by becoming the sole source of emotional sustenance, they can control individuals' emotional well-being. By securing emotional supremacy, they foster dependency, making individuals feel incomplete without their presence, approval, or guidance.

CASE STUDY: THE EMOTIONAL PUPPETEER

Imagine a manipulator who consistently offers unwavering emotional support, becoming the go-to person for validation, advice, and comfort. Over time, you become increasingly reliant on their guidance for your emotional well-being. This emotional supremacy gives them significant influence over your decisions and actions.

NAVIGATING THE TERRAIN

Recognizing the manipulation of securing emotional supremacy is crucial for maintaining your emotional independence. When someone consistently positions themselves as the sole source of emotional support and guidance, it's important to diversify your support network. Value relationships that encourage emotional growth and autonomy while respecting your individual needs.

In Law 40, understanding how manipulators secure emotional supremacy empowers you to engage in relationships with a strong sense of self-reliance. By cultivating a well-rounded support system, nurturing your emotional well-being, and valuing relationships that encourage independence, you can navigate interactions with a healthy balance of emotional influence, rather than being ensnared by manipulative attempts to secure emotional supremacy.

PART X
LAWS FOR ETHICAL CONSIDERATION

LAW 41

EVALUATING INTENTIONS AND CONSEQUENCES

In Law 41, we're exploring the importance of evaluating intentions and consequences in relationships. To navigate the complex dynamics of interactions, it's crucial to assess both the motivations behind actions and the potential outcomes they may yield.

UNDERSTANDING THE PRINCIPLE

Evaluating intentions involves discerning why someone is behaving in a certain way. It requires considering their goals, desires, and underlying motives. On the other hand, evaluating consequences entails examining the potential results of actions, both immediate and long-term, for all parties involved.

BALANCING ACT

Balancing the evaluation of intentions and consequences is essential for maintaining healthy relationships. While understanding someone's intentions can provide insight into their perspectives, recognizing the potential outcomes of actions helps you make informed decisions that align with your values and needs.

CASE STUDY: BALANCING ACT

Imagine a situation where a colleague offers to help you with a project. Their intention might be to showcase their competence and gain recognition. However, the consequence could be that your contributions are overshadowed. By evaluating both their intention and the potential consequence, you can decide how to proceed while considering your own goals.

NAVIGATING THE TERRAIN

In Law 41, understanding the interplay between intentions and consequences empowers you to engage in relationships with mindfulness. By valuing open communication, seeking clarity on motivations, and anticipating potential outcomes, you can navigate interactions with a well-rounded understanding of the dynamics at play. This allows you to make decisions that align with your values and aspirations.

LAW 42

RECOGNIZING AND AVOIDING MANIPULATION

Law 42 focuses on the important skill of identifying and steering clear of manipulation tactics. To safeguard your well-being and maintain healthy relationships, it is important to develop a keen awareness of manipulative tactics and learn strategies to counter them. This will help you protect yourself from being manipulated and ensure that your relationships are based on honesty and mutual respect.

UNDERSTANDING THE PRINCIPLE

Recognizing manipulation involves identifying the tactics and behaviors that manipulators use to control or influence others. Avoiding manipulation requires actively taking steps to protect yourself from falling victim to these tactics and maintaining your autonomy.

EMPOWERING YOURSELF

Empowering yourself to recognize and avoid manipulation is essential for maintaining your agency and emotional well-being. Educate yourself about common manipulative tactics, trust your instincts when something doesn't feel right, and seek external perspectives when in doubt.

CASE STUDY: EMPOWERED CHOICES

Imagine a situation where someone consistently uses guilt to make you comply with their wishes. By recognizing this manipulation, you can respond with assertiveness and set boundaries. Rather than succumbing to guilt, you make empowered choices that align with your desires and values.

NAVIGATING THE TERRAIN

In Law 42, understanding how to recognize and avoid manipulation empowers you to engage in relationships with clarity and self-assurance. By valuing open communication, setting healthy boundaries, and seeking support when needed, you can navigate interactions that are rooted in genuine connections and mutual respect, while sidestepping the pitfalls of manipulation.

LAW 43

FOSTERING EMOTIONAL RESILIENCE

In Law 43, we're exploring the concept of fostering emotional resilience. Developing the ability to bounce back from challenges and setbacks is crucial for maintaining your well-being and navigating relationships with strength.

UNDERSTANDING THE PRINCIPLE

Emotional resilience is the capacity to adapt to adversity and effectively cope with stressors. It involves building a strong sense of self, cultivating positive coping strategies, and nurturing your emotional well-being.

EMPOWERING YOURSELF

Empowering yourself with emotional resilience equips you to handle manipulative tactics and maintain your emotional balance. Strengthen your self-esteem, practice self-care, and seek support from trusted individuals who uplift and encourage you.

CASE STUDY: OVERCOMING MANIPULATION

Imagine a manipulator who consistently uses gaslighting to undermine your confidence. With emotional resilience, you're able to trust your instincts and seek validation from reliable sources. Rather than succumbing to self-doubt, you're empowered to confront manipulation with a clear sense of self.

NAVIGATING THE TERRAIN

In Law 43, understanding how to foster emotional resilience empowers you to engage in relationships with a strong sense of self-worth. By valuing your emotional well-being, practicing self-compassion, and surrounding yourself with supportive individuals, you can navigate interactions with resilience and maintain your emotional equilibrium in the face of manipulation.

LAW 44

BUILDING AUTHENTIC CONNECTIONS

Law 44 focuses on the concept of establishing genuine connections with others. To foster meaningful interactions and prevent manipulation, it is crucial to develop authentic relationships that are built on mutual respect, open communication, and shared values.

UNDERSTANDING THE PRINCIPLE

Building authentic connections involves seeking relationships that are founded on honesty, trust, and shared understanding. It requires valuing individuals for who they truly are and fostering connections that encourage personal growth and well-being.

EMPOWERING YOURSELF

Empowering yourself to build authentic connections requires embracing vulnerability, practicing active listening, and being true to your values. By prioritizing meaningful connections over superficial ones, you create a solid foundation for healthy relationships.

CASE STUDY: MEANINGFUL BONDS

Imagine a relationship where you engage in open conversations, respect each other's boundaries, and provide support during challenging times. This authentic connection is built on shared values and mutual respect, making it less susceptible to manipulation.

NAVIGATING THE TERRAIN

In Law 44, understanding how to build authentic connections empowers you to engage in relationships that uplift and enrich your life. By valuing honesty, respecting boundaries, and seeking connections that encourage growth and well-being, you can navigate interactions with authenticity and create a network of relationships that are grounded in mutual trust and genuine care.

LAW 45

PROMOTING EMOTIONAL INTELLIGENCE

In Law 45, we're exploring the significance of promoting emotional intelligence. Developing the ability to understand, manage, and navigate emotions not only enhances your well-being but also equips you to engage in relationships with empathy and discernment.

UNDERSTANDING THE PRINCIPLE

Emotional intelligence involves recognizing and effectively managing your own emotions while also understanding and empathizing with the emotions of others. It includes self-awareness, self-regulation, social awareness, and relationship management.

EMPOWERING YOURSELF

Empowering yourself with emotional intelligence enables you to accurately perceive emotions, manage stress, and foster healthy relationships. By practicing self-reflection, actively listening to others, and cultivating empathy, you navigate interactions with heightened emotional awareness.

CASE STUDY: EMPATHETIC ENGAGEMENT

Imagine a situation where a friend is struggling with a challenge. With emotional intelligence, you're able to offer genuine support and empathy. Instead of dismissing their emotions, you engage in active listening, providing a safe space for them to share their feelings.

NAVIGATING THE TERRAIN

In Law 45, understanding how to promote emotional intelligence empowers you to engage in relationships with empathy and discernment. By valuing self-awareness, empathetic communication, and emotional well-being, you can navigate interactions that are rooted in understanding, connection, and mutual respect, while effectively identifying and addressing manipulative behaviors.

PART XI
LAWS FOR EMPOWERMENT

LAW 46

ASSERTING PERSONAL BOUNDARIES

Law 46 focuses on the significance of establishing and asserting personal boundaries. It is important to establish and clearly express your boundaries to protect your emotional health, avoid being manipulated, and cultivate positive and balanced relationships.

UNDERSTANDING THE PRINCIPLE

Personal boundaries refer to the limits, both emotional and physical, that individuals establish within their relationships. These boundaries serve as guidelines for how individuals expect to be treated and what they are comfortable with in terms of their personal space and emotional well-being. Boundaries are a way to express your personal preferences and establish what is and isn't acceptable to you in communication. When you assert boundaries, you are establishing limits that help you create a safe environment for yourself and maintain your independence.

EMPOWERING YOURSELF

Empowering yourself to assert personal boundaries requires self-awareness, clear communication, and the willingness to prioritize your well-being. By openly discussing your boundaries, you set the tone for mutual respect and ensure that your needs are met.

CASE STUDY: HONORING BOUNDARIES

Imagine a situation where a colleague consistently invades your personal space. By asserting your boundary and kindly requesting more space, you communicate your comfort level. This empowers you to create a workplace environment that respects your needs.

NAVIGATING THE TERRAIN

In Law 46, understanding how to assert personal boundaries empowers you to engage in relationships with self-respect and integrity. By valuing your emotional and physical well-being, communicating boundaries with clarity, and being assertive when necessary, you can navigate interactions that are grounded in mutual respect and safeguarded against manipulation.

LAW 47

CULTIVATING SELF-AWARENESS

Law 47 delves into the importance of developing self-awareness and its implications. When you take the time to truly understand your thoughts, emotions, and behaviors, it gives you the power to navigate relationships genuinely, make well-informed decisions, and safeguard yourself from being manipulated.

UNDERSTANDING THE PRINCIPLE

Self-awareness involves introspection and reflection to gain insights into your beliefs, emotions, triggers, and patterns. It allows you to recognize your strengths, limitations, and areas for personal growth.

EMPOWERING YOURSELF

Empowering yourself with self-awareness requires mindfulness, self-reflection, and the willingness to confront your thoughts and feelings. By acknowledging your emotions and understanding their origins, you gain the ability to respond to situations in a way that aligns with your values.

CASE STUDY: MINDFUL INTERACTION

Imagine a situation where someone attempts to manipulate you by triggering your insecurities. With self-awareness, you recognize the trigger and understand how it affects your emotions. This awareness empowers you to respond from a place of emotional stability rather than reacting impulsively.

NAVIGATING THE TERRAIN

In Law 47, understanding how to cultivate self-awareness empowers you to engage in relationships with clarity and authenticity. By valuing introspection, embracing your emotions, and seeking personal growth, you can navigate interactions with a heightened awareness of your dynamics, strengths, and vulnerabilities. This self-awareness acts as a shield against manipulation and guides you toward making choices that resonate with your true self.

LAW 48

CHOOSING EMPATHY OVER MANIPULATION

Law 48 explores the concept of how choosing empathy instead of manipulation can have a transformative effect. When you prioritize genuine understanding and compassion in your interactions, it means that you make an effort to truly comprehend others and show empathy towards them. This approach helps to build healthy relationships where both parties feel valued and supported. It also creates an environment that promotes mutual growth, as understanding and compassion allow for open communication and the exchange of ideas. Ultimately, prioritizing these qualities contributes to a more harmonious world, where people can connect on a deeper level and work together towards common goals.

UNDERSTANDING THE PRINCIPLE

Choosing empathy involves making a conscious effort to truly comprehend and establish a deep emotional connection with others. Empathy is the act of understanding and sharing the feelings of others. It requires us to imagine ourselves in their position, actively listen to their experiences without forming any negative opinions, and respond with kindness and understanding.

EMPOWERING YOURSELF

Empowering yourself to choose empathy over manipulation requires a shift in perspective. By valuing authentic connections, embracing vulnerability, and genuinely caring about the well-being of others, you create an environment that is resistant to manipulative tactics.

CASE STUDY: COMPASSIONATE RESPONSE

Imagine a situation where someone makes a mistake and is met with harsh criticism. By choosing empathy, you recognize their humanity and the emotions they might be experiencing. Instead of using their vulnerability against them, you respond with understanding and support.

NAVIGATING THE TERRAIN

In Law 48, understanding how to choose empathy over manipulation empowers you to engage in relationships that elevate both you and others. By valuing authentic connections, fostering open communication, and seeking to understand before seeking to influence, you can navigate interactions with a compassionate and caring spirit, contributing to a world that thrives on genuine connections rather than manipulative tactics.

The End

www.ingramcontent.com/pod-product-compliance
Lightning Source LLC
Chambersburg PA
CBHW060411290526
45791CB00002B/705